FREELANCE 101

SUBHASH CHAUDHARY

Made with ♥ on the Notion Press Platform
www.notionpress.com

To all the freelancers out there, who have taken the plunge and trusted in their own abilities to pursue their dreams.

To those who have found success, and to those who haven't yet – your courage and dedication to the craft is inspiring.

To the clients who choose to work with freelancers, thank you for recognizing the value that freelancers bring to your projects. You are the key to the success of the freelance economy.

Finally, to the countless online communities, platforms, and organizations that have been built to support freelancers. You are the lifeblood of the freelance industry, and we are grateful for your contributions.

Here's to everyone who is part of this ever-growing freelance movement – thank you for your dedication and commitment to the cause.

Contents

Foreword

Freelancing is a growing and powerful phenomenon that is dramatically changing the way people are working in the 21st century.

It is an exciting and liberating way to make a living and to live life on your own terms. This book is a guide to help you get started in freelancing, whether you are just starting out or are an experienced freelancer.

It covers a wide range of topics related to freelancing, from finding work to managing clients, and from setting rates to promoting yourself. This book is packed with practical advice and tips that will help you succeed in freelancing.

It draws on my own experiences as a freelancer and the experiences of many other successful freelancers. I hope that this book provides you with the knowledge and confidence to make the most of your freelancing journey.

Good luck!

Sincerely,

Subhash Chaudhary

Preface

Freelance 101 is the perfect guide for anyone looking to break into the world of freelancing. This book is packed with practical advice and insider tips on how to make freelance work successful.

It covers everything from setting up a business, finding clients, managing finances, and building a portfolio.

This book is written for anyone, whether you're just starting out or have been freelancing for years. Whether you're a full-time freelancer or looking to supplement your income, this book is for you. You don't need to have any prior knowledge or experience to benefit from this book.

We'll start at the beginning and cover everything you need to know about freelancing. We'll go into detail about how to get started, how to find clients, and how to be successful.

This book will help you make the transition from employment to self-employment easier. With the insights and advice provided, you'll be able to make the most of your freelance business.

We hope this book serves as a valuable resource to you as you start or continue your journey in the world of freelancing. Good luck!

Acknowledgements

I would like to express my deepest gratitude to all the people who have helped me throughout the process of writing this book.

First and foremost, I would like to thank my family and friends who have been my biggest support system throughout this journey.

I would also like to thank my editor, Uttam, for their hard work, guidance, and patience.

I would also like to thank the freelancing community for all the advice, support and encouragement that I have received through the years.

Finally, I want to thank all the readers for taking the time to read my work and for inspiring me to pursue my passion.

Prologue

Freelancing is an increasingly popular career option for people across the world. The freedom it provides, the flexible working hours and the ability to work from anywhere are just some of the many advantages of being a freelancer.

In this book, Freelance 101, I will provide an in-depth guide to the world of freelancing. You'll learn how to get started in this exciting career path and how to make the most of it. You'll also learn how to prevent common pitfalls, find the best clients and make a successful career out of freelancing. Whether you're a complete beginner or an experienced freelancer, this book will give you the tools you need to make your freelancing journey a success.

CHAPTER I

What is Freelancing?

Freelancing is a type of self-employment where a person provides services to clients on a contractual basis. The services provided can range from graphic design, writing, and web development, to photography, consulting, and more.

Freelancers usually have the freedom to choose their own hours, work from wherever they want, and set their own rates. Freelancing can be a great option for people who want to be their own boss, work remotely, or make extra money.

It's also an attractive option for people who are looking for more flexibility and control over their careers. There are many advantages to freelancing, including the freedom to choose your own hours and work environment, the potential to earn more money than a traditional job, and the ability to work with a variety of clients.

Freelancing has become a popular and viable option for those looking to supplement or replace traditional employment. But what exactly is freelancing? In its simplest form, freelancing is the act of providing services to clients without the expectation of long-term employment or commitment. Freelancers can offer services such as writing, web design, graphic design, consulting, and more.

The beauty of freelancing is that it allows you to be your own boss and make your own hours. You can pick and choose which jobs you take on and how much you charge for them. You will be responsible for managing your own workload and marketing your services, but you will also have the freedom to work from anywhere and create your own schedule.

There are many benefits to becoming a freelancer. You can gain independence, flexibility, and the opportunity to work on projects that you are passionate about. You can also grow your professional network and increase your chances of success by making yourself more marketable to potential clients. The downside of freelancing is that you don't always have the security of a steady paycheck. You have to be prepared to invest time and money into marketing your services and building a portfolio of clients.

You also have to be able to manage your own finances and handle the paperwork associated with running a business. Overall, freelancing is a great way to make a living while also having the freedom to pursue your passions. With the right attitude and dedication, you can be successful as a freelancer and create an income that meets your needs.

CHAPTER II

Getting Started

If you're new to freelancing, it can be daunting to know where to start. The good news is that getting started is not as difficult as you might think.

Here are some tips to get you started on the right foot.

1. Choose a Niche: It's important to decide what type of services you'd like to offer. Choose a niche that you're knowledgeable and passionate about.

2. Create a Portfolio: A portfolio is a great way to showcase your work and demonstrate your skills. It can include samples of your work, case studies, or references from clients.

3. Set Your Rates: Determine how much you'd like to charge for your services. Research your competitors to get an idea of what the market rate is.

4. Get the Word Out: Create a website, join a freelancing platform, or start networking to find clients.

5. Stay Organized: Establish a system for tracking your finances, invoices, and client contacts.

Identify Your Goals and Objectives

Now that you've laid the groundwork for your freelance business, it's time to start setting some goals and objectives.

This is an essential part of the process, as it will help you stay focused and motivated. When it comes to goal setting, it's important to be realistic. Set goals that are achievable and within reach. Don't set yourself up for failure by setting a goal that's too ambitious or unrealistic.

Start by identifying your long-term career goals. What do you want to accomplish in the next 5 years? Do you want to make a certain amount of money? Do you want to be a sought-after freelancer in your field? Once you've identified your long-term goals, it's time to start setting some short-term goals.

These should be goals that you can reach within the next year, such as increasing your income, building your portfolio, or establishing yourself as an expert in your field. It's also important to set objectives for how you're going to reach these goals. What steps will you take to achieve them? What skills do you need to develop? What resources do you need to acquire? By setting realistic goals and objectives, you can ensure that you stay focused and motivated.

It's also important to regularly review and adjust your goals and objectives as needed. As your business grows and evolves, so too should your goals and objectives.

By following this process, you'll be able to identify and reach your goals quickly and efficiently. Good luck!

Analyze Your Strengths and Weaknesses

Now that you have a good understanding of the freelancing landscape and the types of work available to you, it's time to take a step back and evaluate your own strengths and weaknesses. This is an important step in determining which areas of freelancing will be the most successful for you. First, take some time to make a list of your skills and talents. This can include anything from technical knowledge to communication and problem solving skills.

Once you have a list, think about how those skills could be applied to the types of work available to freelancers. Next, make a list of your weaknesses. This could include areas where you lack knowledge or experience, as well as any personal traits that might make freelancing more difficult for you.

Once you have both lists, review them carefully and identify any areas where you have an advantage or disadvantage. This will help you narrow down the types of work that you are best suited for.

Finally, look at the market and determine which types of jobs are currently in demand. This will help you decide which skills and talents to focus on in order to maximize your success as a freelancer. Analyzing your strengths and weaknesses is a critical step in starting a successful freelancing career.

Taking the time to do this now will help you to find the right types of work and maximize your chances of success in the future.

CHAPTER III

Finding Clients

As a freelancer, the most important part of your business is finding and retaining clients. Without clients, you won't make any money. With that in mind, it's important to have a plan for finding and securing clients.

Here are a few tips for finding clients:

1. Network: One of the best ways to find clients is to network. Reach out to people you know, including friends, family, former colleagues, and classmates. You can also join professional associations and attend networking events.

2. Online Platforms: There are many online platforms that allow freelancers to connect with potential clients. These include websites such as Upwork, Fiverr, and Freelancer.com. These platforms allow you to create a profile and bid on projects.

3. Cold Outreach: Cold outreach involves reaching out to potential clients directly. This can be done through email, social media, or even cold calls. When doing this, it's important to be professional and polite.

4. Online Presence: Having an online presence can help you find clients. This includes having a website, blog, and social media accounts. You can use these to showcase your work, build relationships, and attract potential clients.

5. Referrals: Referrals can be a great way to find clients. Ask your current clients if they know anyone who might need your services. You can also offer incentives, such as discounts, to encourage referrals. These are just a few tips for finding clients as a freelancer.

You can find and secure clients for your business with the right strategies.

CHAPTER IV

Building Your Portfolio

Having a strong portfolio is key to succeeding as a freelancer. It is the best way to showcase your skills and demonstrate how you can help potential clients. Here are some tips for building an impressive portfolio.

1. Choose Your Platform When it comes to creating a portfolio, you have many options. You can create a website, use a portfolio platform such as Behance or Coroflot, or even create a personal blog. It may take some time to decide which platform works best for you, so take the time to research your options and find the one that suits your needs.

2. Showcase Your Work Once you've chosen your platform, it's time to start showing off your work. Choose the projects that best demonstrate your skills and experience, and be sure to include some details about each project. You should also include any testimonials or reviews you've received.

3. Promote Yourself Once your portfolio is up and running, promote it as much as you can. Share it on social media, reach out to potential clients, and don't forget to include a link to your portfolio in your emails.

4. Keep it Updated As you get more projects and gain more experience, be sure to keep your portfolio updated. You want to make sure potential clients see the latest and greatest of your work.

With these tips, you'll be well on your way to creating a portfolio that will attract new clients and help you grow your freelance business. Good luck!

Focus on Quality

In the world of freelancing, quality is king. It's the number one factor that will set you apart from the competition and ensure your success.

As a freelancer, you should always strive to deliver high-quality work that meets or exceeds the expectations of clients.

When it comes to quality, there are a few tips you should keep in mind. First, make sure you thoroughly understand the project requirements and any related deadlines.

Don't be afraid to ask questions or seek clarification if something is unclear.

Second, be sure to communicate with the client throughout the project. Regular check-ins can help ensure that all expectations are met.

Third, use the best tools and resources available to you. Invest in high-quality software, tools, and materials to ensure that your work is of the highest caliber.

Finally, take the time to review your work before submitting it. Make sure it's free of any errors or omissions and that it meets the client's expectations.

Quality control checks can help you ensure that you've done your best work and that the finished product is something you can be proud of. Quality control checks are also important for maintaining a good reputation with clients and potential clients.

By focusing on quality, you can stand out from the competition and ensure that your work is of the highest caliber.

Quality isn't something that can be taken for granted, so make sure that you take the necessary steps to ensure that your work is always top-notch.

CHAPTER V

Setting Your Rates

When it comes to freelancing, one of the most important decisions you will make is setting your rates. A rate that is too low can leave you feeling undervalued, while a rate that is too high could mean that you are not competitive in the marketplace.

It is important to consider the scope of the project, the expected outcomes, the amount of hours you will need to commit to the project and the complexity of the work.

Once you have taken these factors into consideration, you can determine a rate that is fair and reasonable. When starting out, you may want to offer a lower rate as a way of establishing yourself in the industry. Over time, as you gain more experience and expertise, you can increase your rates accordingly.

When discussing rates with your clients, make sure to be clear about what is included in the rate and any additional costs.

When setting your rates, it is important to also consider the cost of running your business. This includes the cost of taxes, equipment, software, and other overhead expenses. Make sure to factor in the cost of running your business when determining your rate.

Finally, make sure to stay up to date on industry trends and market conditions. This will help you remain competitive in the marketplace and ensure that you are charging a fair and reasonable rate.

By taking the time to research and determine a fair and reasonable rate, you will be able to ensure that you are getting paid what you deserve for your work. Setting your rates is an important part of running a successful freelance business.

CHAPTER VI

Time management

Time management is an essential skill for any freelancer. Managing your time well can help you stay organized, increase your efficiency, and make sure you're meeting deadlines.

Here are some tips to help you manage your time more effectively as a freelancer.

1. Set specific work hours. Having specific work hours is a great way to manage your time. Decide on when you plan to work each day and stick to it. This will help you stay on track and ensure you're not wasting time.

2. Prioritize your tasks. Make a list of all the tasks you need to do and prioritize them according to importance and urgency. This will help you focus on the most important tasks first and avoid procrastination.

3. Break down big tasks. Big tasks can be overwhelming, so it's important to break them down into smaller, more manageable chunks. This will make them easier to complete and help you stay on track.

4. Set realistic deadlines. Setting realistic deadlines is essential for successful time management. Don't set unrealistic deadlines for yourself and make sure you plan for any unexpected delays.

5. Take regular breaks. Taking regular breaks is important for both your physical and mental health. Taking a break to stretch, get some fresh air, or take a few minutes to relax can help you stay focused and productive.

By following these tips, you can improve your time management as a freelancer and ensure you're meeting deadlines, staying organized, and staying productive.

Automate Where Possible

As a freelancer, you are responsible for running your own business. This means taking care of all the administrative tasks yourself, from setting up invoices and tracking payments to managing your own marketing and outreach.

In order to stay on top of your freelance business and maximize efficiency, it is important to automate as much as possible. The first step in automating your freelancing business is to set up a system for tracking payments and invoices.

This can be done through a variety of tools, such as FreshBooks or Wave, that allow you to easily create invoices and keep track of payments.

Additionally, you can set up automated payment reminders to ensure that you get paid on time. The next step is to automate your marketing and outreach efforts.

There are a variety of tools available that can help you create and send out automated emails, post to social media, and even keep track of your contacts.

This allows you to focus more of your time on the actual work instead of spending time manually managing your marketing efforts.

Finally, it is important to set up systems for keeping track of your finances and taxes.

This includes setting up a spreadsheet to track income and expenses, as well as setting up automated reminders for filing taxes.

Additionally, there are a variety of online tools, such as QuickBooks, that make it easy to keep track of your finances and taxes.

By automating as much of your freelancing business as possible, you will be able to save time and energy, allowing you to focus on the actual work that you do.

With the right tools, you can make sure that you stay ahead of the game and maximize efficiency in your business.

CHAPTER VII

Staying Motivated

Freelancing can be an isolating experience, especially when working from home. It's easy to get overwhelmed and discouraged when you're not seeing the results you're hoping for, so it's important to stay motivated and have a positive attitude.

Here are a few tips to help you stay motivated while freelancing:

Create a Schedule: Establishing a daily schedule and sticking to it can help you stay focused and productive. Having a set routine also allows for more work/life balance, which can help reduce stress and burnout.

Set Achievable Goals: It's important to set realistic goals for yourself and break them down into smaller, achievable tasks. Give yourself smaller rewards for each task you complete along the way, and celebrate when you achieve your larger goals.

Network: Don't forget to reach out to other freelancers for advice, tips, and support. Networking with other freelancers can help you stay motivated and provide you with a sense of community.

Find Inspiration: Take time to explore and find motivation in unexpected places. Try learning something new, reading a book, or taking a class to spark creativity.

Take Breaks: Working long hours can be exhausting, so make sure to take regular breaks throughout the day. Taking a break can help you refocus and be more productive.

Stay Positive: Don't get discouraged by failure. Instead, focus on the things you've accomplished, and don't forget to pat yourself on the back for a job well done.

Freelancing can be a great way to make money and have more control over your work. With the right attitude and motivation, you can be successful in your freelance career.

CHAPTER VIII

Networking

One of the most important aspects of freelancing is networking. As a freelancer, you must be able to develop and maintain long-lasting connections with other professionals in your industry. This is essential for finding new clients, staying up-to-date with industry trends, and developing a competitive edge.

Let's start with what networking actually is. Networking is building and maintaining relationships with other professionals or people with a common interest or goal. Networking is essential for any freelancer, because it can open up new opportunities and help you stay ahead of the competition.

Now that we've established the importance of networking, let's discuss some effective ways to network as a freelancer.

1. Attend industry events. Attending industry events is one of the best ways to network. These events are often filled with other professionals who are looking to make new connections and build their own networks.

2. Join online groups. There are many online groups that are specifically geared towards freelancers. Joining these groups can be a great way to connect with other professionals and build your network.

3. Reach out to potential clients. Reaching out to potential clients is a great way to network. You can use email, social media, or even cold calling to introduce yourself and explain your services.

4. Leverage social media. Social media is a great tool for freelancers. You can use platforms such as Twitter and LinkedIn to connect with other professionals and build your network.

5. Join professional organizations. Joining professional organizations is another great way to network. You will be able to attend events and meet other professionals in your industry.

These are just a few of the many ways to network as a freelancer. Be sure to take advantage of all the opportunities available to expand and strengthen your network. Networking is an essential part of freelancing, so don't neglect it!

CHAPTER IX

Conclusion

As you have learned from Freelance 101, freelancing can be a great way to make money, gain experience, and gain independence.

It is important to remember to research the industry, network, use the right tools, and set realistic goals while building your freelance business.

Freelancing is not without its drawbacks. It can be challenging to juggle multiple projects and clients at once, and there can be times when you don't have any work coming in.

It is important to have a good budgeting system and plan ahead for these lean times.

Also, remember to take time for yourself and your loved ones. Working too many hours can be detrimental to your mental and physical health.

Make sure you are taking breaks, getting enough sleep, and eating healthy. It is also important to be aware of the legal aspects of freelancing. It is essential to understand the laws governing employment, taxes, and contracts.

With dedication and hard work, you can make a successful career out of freelancing. It is a great way to gain independence and make money. Good luck as you start your journey as a freelancer!

9 798888 838563

Printed by Libri Plureos GmbH in Hamburg, Germany